F5
WARPLANE FOR THE WORLD

Robbie Shaw

Airlife
England

ACKNOWLEDGEMENTS

To illustrate an F-5 from every country which has operated the type is impossible, as many third world countries for some reason simply do not allow photography of even civil aircraft, let alone military ones. Fortunately in the West most countries are helpful, and with the exception of the Greek Air Force who were totally obstructive as usual, I would like to thank those in North America and Europe for their assistance — in particular, thanks must go to the Canadian Armed Forces and the Spanish Air Force for being especially helpful.

I am also grateful to those who lent material for use in this publication, in particular Maurice Bertrand, Peter Foster, David Oliver, Chris Pocock, Pete Smith and the PR department at Northrop.

Unless otherwise credited, all photographs were taken by the author using Kodachrome film.

ABBREVIATIONS

AAM	Air to Air Missile	RJAF	Royal Jordanian Air Force
AB	Air Base	RNLAF	Royal Netherlands Air Force
ACMI	Air Combat Manoeuvring Instrumentation	RNoAF	Royal Norwegian Air Force
AETE	Aerospace Engineering and Test Establishment	ROCAF	Republic of China Air Force
AFB	Air Force Base	ROKAF	Republic of Korea Air Force
AIDC	Aero Industry Development Centre	RSAF	Royal Saudi Air Force
AS	Aggressor Squadron	SVNAF	South Vietnamese Air Force
CAF	Canadian Armed Forces	TAC	Tactical Air Command
CCTS	Combat Crew Training Squadron	TFTAS	Tactical Fighter Training Aggressor Squadron
CFFTS	Canadian Forces Flying Training School	TFTS	Tactical Fighter Training Squadron
CW	Composite Wing	TFW	Tactical Fighter Wing
DACT	Dissimilar Air Combat Training	TNI-AU	Tentara Nasional Indonesia – Angkatan Udara
FAB	Forca Aerea Brasileira	TTW	Tactical Training Wing
FAC	Fuerza Aerea de Chile	TUDM	Tentara Udara Diraja Malaysia
FAM	Fuerza Aerea Mexicana	USAF	United States Air Force
FW	Fighter Wing	USMC	United States Marine Corps
FWS	Fighter Weapons School	USN	United States Navy
IIAF	Imperial Iranian Air Force	VF	Naval Fighter Squadron
LEX	Leading Edge Extension	VFA	Naval Fighter Attack Squadron
MAP	Military Assistance Programme	VHF	Very High Frequency
RCAF	Royal Canadian Air Force	VMFT	Marine Fighter Training Squadron

Copyright © Robbie Shaw, 1990

First published in the UK in 1990 by Airlife Publishing Ltd.

British Cataloguing in Publication Data available.

ISBN 1 85310 136 2 (Hardback)
ISBN 1 85310 111 7 (Paperback)

Airlife Publishing Ltd.

101 Longden Road, Shrewsbury SY3 9EB, England.

INTRODUCTION

On 10 July 1989, only a few weeks short of the thirtieth anniversary of the first flight of the Northrop F-5, three passed through Prestwick on delivery from Palmdale, California en-route to the Republic of Singapore Air Force. These were the last of nearly 3,000 F-5s to be delivered, thereby ending a production run of exceptional length for a modern warplane.

The story of the F-5 began back in the 1950s, when Northrop was one of a number of manufacturers looking to develop a simple, cheap, lightweight fighter. In 1955 the company proposed its project, the N156 series, with seven configurations, including a carrier-borne variant. The N156T two seat tandem trainer was the first success — subject to successful flight tests, and was selected by the USAF's Air Training Command as a T-33 replacement. The aircraft took to the air for the first time on 10 April 1959, and was soon in production as the T-38 Talon. Almost 1,200 Talons were built, not only for the USAF, but the US Navy and NASA received small numbers, whilst some were exported under the Military Assistance Programme (MAP).

The 425 TFTS was initially a component of the Luke-based 58 TTW, later transferring to the 405 TTW, also based at Luke. The F-5s therefore were frequent visitors to Luke AFB, where this E model was photographed alongside an F-15 from a sister unit in the 405 TTW.

The N156F proposal was for a single seat lightweight fighter with two fuselage-mounted afterburning engines. The design was virtually identical to the Talon and had the same wing span. The wing had leading edge extension (LEX) and removable wing tip fuel tanks. To reduce the landing roll a brake parachute was fitted, as was an arrester hook for emergencies. Primary armament consisted of two 20mm M-39 cannons, and an AIM-9 Sidewinder air to air missile (AAM) on each wingtip — if no tip tanks were carried. Centreline and two wing mounted pylons could be used to carry an assortment of rockets, bombs or long range fuel tanks.

The company received the go-ahead in 1958 to produce three prototypes and a static test airframe. By the time of its maiden flight on 30 July 1959, only four months after that of its sister aircraft, the T-38 Talon, the N156F had been named Freedom Fighter. Further improvements to make the type truly multi-role included an additional internal fuel tank for added range, and a reconnaissance pack in an interchangeable nose cone. This version was known as the N156C. It also incorporated a strengthened wing to enable external loads to be carried on four wing pylons, instead of the two originally planned.

The N156C variant was selected by the U.S. Department of Defense in 1962 for issue under MAP to friendly governments, usually on extremely attractive credit terms, or even being underwritten completely by the U.S. The type was given the designation F-5 in August 1962, and the first order for seventy-one aircraft was received two months later.

First production F-5As were powered by two General Electric J85-13 turbojets with afterburner, each producing 4,080lb (1,850kg) thrust. These were delivered to the 4441st Combat Crew Training Squadron (CCTS) at Williams AFB, Arizona, which was set up to train the crews of the countries about to receive the Northrop jet. First recipient was the Imperial Iranian Air Force (IIAF), quickly followed by the Republic of Korea Air Force (ROKAF). These two air arms soon built up a large complement of the Northrop fighter. Deliveries were not confined to the Third World however, and very soon the NATO partners Greece and Turkey took delivery of their first batches simultaneously. The air forces of Ethiopia, Libya, Morocco, Norway, Philippines, Taiwan, Thailand, and South Vietnam soon joined the F-5 club, the latter blooding the aircraft in combat. The delivery to Libya of eight A and two B models occurred prior to the military coup of 1969 which brought Col. Gaddafi to power, and it has been reported that these aircraft were loaned to Pakistan during its war against India in 1971. The current status of these aircraft is unknown. The last of 617 F-5As produced by Northrop was delivered in 1972.

Bottom: Rather surprisingly for a training unit, the variant of the F-5 operated in least numbers by the 425th with the F-5F. This F-5F is also wearing Royal Saudi Air Force insignia, as Saudi pilots were 'borrowing' 425th aircraft to participate in a Red Flag exercise at Nellis. *(GB Aircraft Slides)*

Below: Over the years Williams F-5s have worn a variety of colour schemes. This 425th F-5E is wearing the 'Vietnam' type camouflage pattern prevalent in Tactical Air Command at the time, and the 'LA' tailcode allocated to the 405 TTW. *(GB Aircraft Slides)*

To complement the F-5A, a two seat trainer F-5B variant was quickly put into production. Almost identical to the T-38, the B model had the same tandem seating arrangement, with the rear seat raised by ten inches. The gun armament was removed from this variant, which has proved to be a drawback from an operational training point of view. The first flight of the F-5B was on 24 February 1964, and deliveries commenced soon afterwards to the growing band of operators. The training unit at Williams changed designation to the 425th Tactical Fighter Training Squadron (TFTS) belonging to the 405th Tactical Training Wing (TTW). The squadron continued training F-5 pilots for many countries until its disbandment early in 1989. A total of 183 B models were produced by Northrop's Palmdale facility, with the last deliveries to the ROKAF in the mid 1970s.

The first of eighty-nine RF-5A reconnaissance variants built was delivered in the late 1960s. The first customer again was the IIAF, followed by the air forces of Greece, Morocco, Norway, South Korea, South Vietnam, Thailand and Turkey.

License production of the F-5 was the next development for Northrop's worldwide fighter. The Spanish Air Force selected the F-5 to start a modernisation programme, with an order for seventy aircraft, and Northrop came to an agreement with Construcciones Aeronauticas S.A. (CASA). The first eight machines were built by Northrop, and the remainder of the order was supplied in component form to CASA for assembly at its Seville and Getafe plants. The order comprised thirty-four SF-5B, and eighteen each of the SF-5A and SRF-5A versions, with deliveries commencing in June 1968.

Another license agreement was made with Canadair after the Royal Canadian Air Force selected the F-5, its first choice, the F-4 Phantom, being too expensive. The CF-5 as it was known by Canadair, differed in many respects from its Northrop counterpart. It was powered by General Electric J85-15 engines license-built by Orenda. These were slightly more powerful than the U.S. built powerplants, and other alterations included the necessary de-icing equipment, and a more advanced avionics fit. They were also fitted with the necessary pipes and plumbing for air to air refuelling, via a removable probe to be fitted to the forward fuselage on the starboard side just forward of the canopy. Total production for the Canadians was eighty-nine CF-5A, and forty-six CF-5D two seaters. These were given the designation CF-116 by the CAF. Due to defence cuts during the manufacture of these aircraft a number became surplus to Canadian requirements, and sixteen CF-5A, and four CF-5Ds were sold to the Venezuelan Air Force. Canadair also produced 105 NF-5 Freedom Fighters for the Royal Netherlands Air Force as replacements for their ageing F-84F Thunderstreaks. This order comprised seventy-five A, and thirty B, models with deliveries commencing in November 1969.

Following the success of its Freedom Fighter, it was only a matter of time before Northrop developed an improved version. Powerplant selected was the General Electric J85-21 with 5,000lb (2,240kg) thrust, and to accommodate this larger engine the fuselage was widened by sixteen inches, whilst the length of the aircraft was increased by fifteen inches. Wing span was also extended by seventeen inches to twenty-six feet and eight inches. The wing also incorporated leading edge flaps for improved manoeuvrability, an idea borrowed from the Dutch F-5s built by Canadair. Another feature taken from Canadair built aircraft was the provision of a two position nosewheel leg, which could be raised on the ground by three degrees. This angle of attack provided more lift over the wings, and resulted in the take-off run being decreased by some twenty to thirty per cent. Other improvements included an Emerson APQ-153 radar and improved avionics, and, if required by the customer, a Litton LN-33 inertial navigation system. This variant was put forward by the company and was selected as the winner in a Department of Defense competition for an International Fighter Aircraft. Designated the F-5E Tiger II (the SVNAF already used the name Tiger for their F-5A/Bs), the prototype took to the air on 11 August 1972.

For over thirty years the international school for F-5 pilots, the 425 TFTS operated from Williams AFB, Arizona. The unit phased out its F-5As in the early 1970s in favour of the E model, but the two seat Bs soldiered on into the '80s. Illustrated is an F-5E in the high visibility scheme worn in the '70s. *(Author's collection)*

Due to the difference in performance between the A and E models, it was soon realised that the two seat F-5B was far from ideal in training pilots for the more powerful F-5E, so a trainer derivative of the E was required. This was done simply by stretching the forward fuselage by forty-two inches, and thus the F-5F was born. Unlike the F-5B gun armament was retained, with a single M-39 cannon located in the forward port fuselage. A total of 194 F-5F's were rolled out from the Palmdale plant.

License production of the F-5E/F was undertaken in three countries. The Republic of China Air Force was already an experienced operator of both the F-5A/B models, and was an early customer for the F-5E, ordering an initial batch of sixty in 1975. Taiwan's Aero Industry Development Centre (AIDC) set up a production line to produce under license both the F-5E and F models, named Chung Cheng by the ROCAF. Production ceased in 1988 after 242 E, and sixty-six F models had been built. In 1975 the Swiss Air Force selected the Tiger II to replace its ageing fleet of Venoms, and initially ordered sixty-six E and six F models. The first thirteen Es and all six Fs were built by Northrop, the remainder were assembled locally by the Federal Aircraft Factory at Emmen. A repeat order for thirty-two E and six F variants was completed in Switzerland. South Korea, another established F-5 operator, set up production of the Tiger II in 1981, and produced forty-eight single seat F-5Es, and twenty F-5F trainer versions. These aircraft were produced by Korean Air at its Kimhae factory, and the type is named Chegoong-Ho (Air Master) by the ROKAF.

Initial deliveries once again went to 425 TFTS at Williams, quickly followed by large numbers to the ROKAF and SVNAF. Over 100 Tiger IIs had been delivered to the latter by the time of the fall of South Vietnam, and twenty-seven of these, along with sixty F-5A/B models were left behind to the invading North Vietnamese. Many of the aircraft which were recovered, and those on the Northrop production for the SVNAF were eventually transferred to the USAF and USN inventories, where they formed 'aggressor squadrons'. Northrop was convinced that many customers for the earlier F-5A would be interested in the vastly improved F-5E, and so it proved to be, as the air forces of Ethiopia, Iran, Morocco, Taiwan and Thailand ordered Tiger IIs. For the next fifteen years the busy Northrop production line produced aircraft for a host of new customers, such as Saudi Arabia, Jordan, Malaysia, Brazil, Chile, North Yemen, Switzerland, Kenya, Singapore, Indonesia, Mexico, Sudan, Tunisia and Bahrain. Total F-5E production by Northrop was 1,003.

The final variant of the F-5 series to enter production was the RF-5E Tigereye. Easily distinguishable from the rest of the family, the Tigereye has an elongated nose with windows for a variety of cameras and sensors. Surprisingly, this adds only eight inches to the overall length. A single M-39 cannon is retained in the nose, as is the capability to carry defensve AAMs. Sales of this variant have however proved to be disappointing, total production running to just twelve aircraft; two for Malaysia and ten for Saudi Arabia.

Mention must also be made of the final, albeit briefly, member of the F-5 series, the F-5G Tigershark. In 1980 Northrop began construction of the type which was based primarily on the F-5E, but powered by a single General Electric F404 turbofan producing 18,000lb (8,000kg) thrust. A larger tail and strengthened wing were complemented by a larger canopy for improved visibility — essential for air to air combat. Shortly before its first flight on 30 August 1982, the aircraft was redesignated F-20 — probably for marketing reasons, to show it was not just another F-5! Very quickly the aircraft impressed those involved in the flight test programme as it exceeded Mach 2 and manoeuvred at 9g. Considerable interest was shown by a number of countries and Bahrain was first to place an order — for four aircraft. This however was insufficient for Northrop to open the production line as the hoped for order to replace the F-5Es in the USAF 'aggressor squadrons' was not forthcoming. The lack of orders from the U.S. military no doubt influenced many air arms who had shown interest in the F-20, and some turned instead to the F-16. Worse was to come, as the prototype was lost in a crash in October 1984 whilst demonstrating the aircraft to ROKAF. Seven months later the second prototype was lost in Canada, the suspected cause being g induced loss of consciousness to the pilot. A year later the third prototype flew, but in the absence of the hoped for orders the programme has fallen into a state of limbo, and it remains to be seen if it will be resurrected at a future date.

With the possible exception of the North American F-86 Sabre, the F-5 has been sold to more countries than any other combat aircraft in the western world, and is on a par with the Soviet built MiG-21. It has been operated by thirty-six air arms in thirty-four countries. In addition to the United States Air Force, Navy and Marine Corps, the following countries are, or have been, F-5 operators: Bahrain, Brazil, Canada, Chile, Ethiopia, Greece, Honduras, Indonesia, Iran, Jordan, Kenya, Libya, Malaysia, Mexico, Morocco, Netherlands, North Yemen, Norway, Pakistan, Philippines, Saudi Arabia, Singapore, South Korea, South Vietnam, Spain, Sudan, Switzerland, Taiwan, Thailand, Tunisia, Turkey, Venezuela and Vietnam.

(Robbie Shaw, January 1990)

AGGRESSORS

During the latter stages of the Vietnam War the USAF and USN became rather disturbed at the poor kill ratio in air to air combat. In stark contrast to the Korean War where a kill ratio of 10:1 was achieved in air to air combat, over Vietnam this was down to 2:1, despite the general superiority of U.S. aircraft. It was felt therefore that U.S. aircrew training could be improved, particularly when statistics proved that the vast majority of U.S. aircrew who were shot down were on their first few missions. The Navy were the first to address the problem by forming an

Below: Of the various colour schemes adopted by the aggressor F-5s the desert camouflage most suited operations over the Nellis ranges. *(Ton van Schaik)*

'aggressor' squadron with T-38 Talons. Although far from ideal, the Talon was chosen due to its size and similar operational characteristics to the main adversary, the Mig-21. The USAF quickly followed suit, initially with the T-38. With the fall of Vietnam, however, there was suddenly a surplus of F-5Es which had been built for the SVNAF, and these more powerful aircraft proved to be an ideal Mig-21 substitute. Staffed with combat veterans from Vietnam, the first Tactical Fighter Training Aggressor Squadrons (TFTAS), the 64th and 65th, were formed under the 57 TTW at Nellis AFB. These squadrons adopted Soviet procedures, the crews were taught to think and act like Russians, and the aircraft adopted a variety of camouflage patterns, including those worn by Soviet Bloc aircraft.

The aggressor squadrons then began to tour many TAC bases, flying dissimilar air combat training (DACT) missions against aircraft such as the F-4, F-15 etc. In addition the aggressor squadrons provided invaluable training during Red Flag exercises, and the USAF were so impressed with the results that a further two squadrons were formed. These were the 26 TFTAS at Clark AB in the Philippines and the 527 TFTAS at Alconbury in the UK, these units providing aggressor training for PACAF and USAFE units respectively. The latter unit also flew against squadrons from other NATO countries. A few years ago the units changed designation from TFTAS to simply Aggressor Squadron (AS), and more recently have begun to convert to the F-16 Fighting Falcon. At the time of writing only the 65 AS remains to convert. Conversion of the F-16 has also meant a change of location for the two overseas units; the 26 AS relocating to Kadena, Okinawa, whilst the 527th made a shorter trip to Bentwaters.

Opposite: A pair of Nellis based aggressors landing at CFB Cold Lake where they were participating in the Maple Flag exercise, which is the Canadian equivalent to Red Flag.

Below: The last two digits of the serial highlighted denote this aircraft as the one allocated to the commander of the 57 TTW. Individual squadron markings are not carried by aircraft of the 64th and 65th Aggressor Squadrons, though the 57 TTW's distinctive black and yellow checks are displayed on the fin.

Below: A rare shot of an F-5F belonging to the 57 TTW.

PACAF REDS

The 26 AS operated the F-5E alongside a small number of T-33s to provide DACT training to PACAF units. Located at Clark AB in the Philippines, home of the 3 TFW, this meant that the unit had to fly considerable distances to reach its 'customers'. The nearest 'hop' was to Kadena AB on Okinawa, home of the 18 TFW. This base was a frequent stopover point en-route to the PACAF bases in Korea and to Misawa in Northern Japan. The complement of the 26th included six F-5Es destined for the Ethiopian Air Force which, due to an embargo, never reached their intended customer. The squadron disposed of its T-33s to the Philippine Air Force in 1987, and moved to Kadena in 1989 ready to equip with the F-16.

Below: Sitting at the holding point at Clark, this 26 AS aircraft awaits the groundcrews for a 'last chance' check. The aircraft is carrying a Sidewinder acquisition round on the port wing tip. Note that the nose is in the raised position for take-off.

Opposite: A 26 AS F-5E on final approach to Clark, where a dormant volcano dominates the skyline.

Below: This 1975 build F-5E was one of the embargoed Ethiopian aircraft. The striking green, brown and tan camouflage pattern was officially known as 'Snake'.

Opposite: Silver painted F-5E proclaiming to be the mount of the 26th Aggressor Commander. Silver was one of the five paint schemes adopted for the aggressor fleet.

Below: Seven aircraft of the 26 AS at rest on the Kadena ramp. The unit had just completed a three-week deployment flying DACT against the based F-15 squadrons. Note the variety of colour schemes.

Opposite: When aggressor F-5s went for major overhaul they rarely came out of the paint shop the same colour as when they went it. It seemed the perfect opportunity to experiment with different shades, such as the three shades of grey on this 26 AS aircraft at Clark.

Below: Insignia of the 26th Aggressor Squadron.

Below: Shades of blue would be an apt title for the attractive scheme of this Clark based aircraft. The Russian style two digit modex on the nose adds to the effect.

YANKEE REDS FOR EUROPE

The last Aggressor Squadron to form was the 527th at RAF Alconbury on the 1st April 1976. Soon afterwards the first batch of eight aircraft arrived courtesy of a C-5 Galaxy, which soon became a regular method of delivering the Northrop fighter. The UK based unit quickly built up to an established strength of twenty aircraft, double that of its PACAF sister unit. Alconbury was home to the RF-4C-equipped 10 TRW, and it was against these aircraft, and F-15s from Bitburg that the unit worked up to

Overleaf: The bulky 275 US gallon fuel tank is necessary to enable the F-5 to reach Decimomannu from Alconbury, with a refuelling stop en-route at Ramstein.

Below: The toned down low visibility markings tend to be difficult to discern amongst the shades of blue on aircraft 01535 of the 527 AS on the taxiway at Alconbury.

operational readiness. Standard fit for aggressor F-5s was an AIM-9 Sidewinder acquisition round on one wingtip, with an Air Combat Manoeuvring Instrumentation (ACMI) pod on the other. The main adversary of the 527th were the F-15 Eagles from Bitburg and Soesterberg, though F-4s and later F-16s spent many an hour dogfighting over the North Sea with the F-5s. Interspersed were RAF Phantom squadrons and fighters from a number of NATO units. Later the squadron set up a semi-permanent detachment at Decimomannu, Sardinia, to make full use of the ACMI range installed there and the opportunity to pit their skills against the many allied aircraft and crews operating from this NATO facility. During 1988 the 527th vacated its Alconbury home for nearby Bentwaters, and became the first of the aggressor units to equip with the F-16C.

Opposite: Taxying clear of the Alconbury runway is a Tiger II in the 'Ghost' colour scheme of grey and blue.

Below: A 527 AS F-5E with long range fuel tank on the runway at Alconbury.

Opposite: Trundling down the Alconbury taxiway is F-5E 01547 in Mig-21 type silver scheme. You can just make out the red star worn on the flying helmets of aggressor pilots.

Below: A rare sight — a pair of 527th aircraft in close formation. In the 'play area' these aircraft would normally be in battle formation, at least 1,000 yards apart.

Opposite: A pair of 527 AS Tiger IIs on final approach to their Alconbury base.

Below: Against a cloudy background this light grey scheme makes this 527th machine almost invisible.

Opposite: The gear retracts as this 527 AS F-5E lifts off from Sculthorpe
for a DACT mission against Spangdahlem based F-4G Phantoms.

Below: Silver '49 flaring for touchdown.

Opposite: The green, brown and tan scheme is officially known as 'Snake'. Aircraft 01551 of the 527 AS was photographed at RAF Wyton.

Below: With an ACMI pod on the starboard wing tip this 527 AS F-5E crosses the Sardinian coast on recovery to Decimomannu.
(Author's collection)

Opposite: Photogenic Tiger II in the 'Snake' camouflage scheme on the taxiway at Alconbury. The squadron used the callsign 'Baron', taken from that well known First World War ace.

Below: With undercarriage retracting, aircraft 01560 climbs out of Alconbury for another encounter over the North Sea. A previous adversary, Eskadron 726 of the Royal Danish Air Force have left their mark in the shape of their unit insignia above the port wing root.

Below: The non-standard European aggressor scheme on this 527th machine could perhaps be explained by the fact it was a recent attrition replacement from Nellis.

RED SAILORS

The USN Fighter Weapons School (FWS) at Miramar initially used T-38 Talons and A-4 Skyhawks for aggressor training. However, shortly after the USAF acquired the F-5E, the Navy did likewise, though in much smaller numbers. A total of ten F-5E and three F models were taken on charge by the Navy, equipping the FWS and VF-126 at Miramar and VF-43 at Oceana. All three units have since disposed of their F-5s in favour of the F-16N, and the Tiger IIs have been passed on to the current operators; VF-45 at Key West and VFA-127 at Fallon. The survivors of the original batch have been topped up by ex-USAF 527 AS aircraft, and the USMC formed its first F-5 aggressor unit, VMFT-401 at Yuma in late 1989, also with ex USAF machines.

Below: This F-5E in an unusual tan and green camouflage belongs to the FWS at Miramar, where it was photographed touching down. This unit now operates the F-16N alongside A-4 Skyhawks in the aggressor role.

Below: Sharing the Oceana ramp with A-6 Intruders and F-14 Tomcats is this F-5E of VF-43 'Challengers'. This unit has since relinquished its Tiger IIs.

CANADA'S
FREEDOM FIGHTERS

The prototype CF-5A first flew in May 1968 from Edwards AFB, California, where the first few Canadair built aircraft carried out flight tests. Although built in Canada, these aircraft were transported to Edwards by Canadian Hercules aircraft. The first to fly in Canada was a CF-5D in August 1968 at Cartierville. First deliveries were to the Aerospace Engineering and Test Establishment at Cold Lake, where initial Canadian trials took place. This unit still operates a few CF-5A and Ds on routine test and chase plane duties. The first squadron to form was 434 'Bluenose' in 1968, and the first batch of pilots went to Williams for training whilst their aircraft were being built. First deliveries reached the squadron at Cold Lake in early 1969, where its first task as

Below: An interesting array of stores on the wing pylon of this CF-5D on the ramp at Cold Lake. The 'X' on the rudder of this aircraft, the first CF-5D built, denotes it belongs to the AETE (the 'X' standing for experimental).

a training unit was to train pilots for the second squadron, No. 433 'Porcupine' to be based at Bagotville. Aircraft from both units undertook their first European deployment in 1970, to Prestwick and Sollingen. Eventually bolt-on refuelling probes were fitted to a number of A models, and two CAF Boeing CC-137s were configured to a convertable passenger/tanker fit. The first European deployment with the aid of air to air refuelling took place in 1973. Number 434 Squadron later joined its sister unit 433 at Bagotville, both units being tasked with ground attack and interdiction, and assigned a NATO role of reinforcing Norway. Simultaneously the training role was undertaken by No. 1 Canadian Forces Flying Training Squadron (CFFTS) at Cold Lake, which was later designated 419 'Moose' Squadron. This squadron is still current, and remains the sole operational CF-5 unit, as 433 Squadron has converted to the CF-18, and 434 Squadron moved briefly to Chatham before disbanding.

Overleaf: After gaining their wings on the CT-114 Tutor, CAF pilots destined for the CF-18 must successfully complete an advanced flying course on the CF-5. Part of the syllabus includes air to air refuelling from the two specially adapted Boeing CC-137s. Here a student approaches the drogue basket trailed from the CC-137, whilst the instructor looks on from a formating CF-5D.

Opposite: In 1989 419 'Moose' Squadron painted this CF-5A in special markings to commemorate a squadron anniversary. Note the Moose painted on the fin. *(CAF)*

Below right: To complement the Moose on the fin, a giant sized Maple leaf adorns the underside of this aircraft. *(CAF)*

Opposite: An impressive shot of an AETE CF-5A during a ground attack training mission. Note the cameras in the reconnaissance nose.
(AETE, CAF)

Below: An AETE CF-5D acting as chase plane formates on a CT-33A.
(Peter Foster)

Opposite: Refuelling to an audience. This CF-5A pilot makes a successful contact whilst the wingman in a two seater looks on.

Below: For those students who have trouble mastering the art of plugging the probe into an oscillating basket during the refuelling phase, doing it by night must be a nerve wracking experience.

Opposite: Number three drops out of formation to take his turn at the drogue basket.

Below: A 433 'Porcupine' Squadron CF-5A tucks in close to the wing of the CC-137 tanker which assisted the deployment of CF-5s from Bagotville to Nellis. The luminous strips are lit to assist pilots in night formation flying, and are very effective.

Opposite: The streamlined fuselage and thin wing are evident in this shot of a CF-5D on the Cold Lake flightline.

Below: Note the dummy canopy painted on the undersides of this aggressor CF-5D of 419 Squadron. This features on CAF CF-18 aircraft also, and helps to confuse an adversary during air to air combat.

Opposite: A gaily coloured CF-5D of 419 Squadron in aggressor markings.

Below: A few CF-5Ds retain their natural metal finish, such as this 419 Squadron machine over the Primrose Lake training area. The serial number 116841 on the fin denotes it is the forty-first CF-5D built. The official CAF designation for the F-5 is the CF-116, and serial numbers of single seaters began with the figure seven, and eight for the two seat D model.

Overleaf: A CF-5A of 433 Squadron about to land at its Bagotville base. For some reason this unit carried the unit badge on the port intake only. This unit currently operates the CF-18 Hornet. *(Peter Foster)*

Opposite: A 419 Squadron CF-5D taxies from the Cold Lake ramp to participate in a Maple Flag exercise. This camouflage scheme is almost identical to the USAF 'Snake' scheme worn on their aggressor F-5s.

Below: Aircraft of 434 Squadron were easily identifiable due to the blue fin band containing a white schooner, and sometimes used the radio callsign 'Schooner Pirates'.

Below: Although fitted with a brake parachute, the pilot of this 434 Squadron CF-5AR has elected not to use it on this occasion, and has kept the nose raised to apply aerodynamic braking during the landing roll at Cold Lake. This photograph was taken in 1984 when the squadron was based at Bagotville but operating from Cold Lake during a Maple Flag exercise.

THE F-5 IN EUROPE:
THE NETHERLANDS

The Royal Netherlands Air Force (RNLAF) selected the Canadair built F-5 to replace its ageing fleet of F-84 Thunderstreaks. These were designated NF-5s, and seventy-five single, and thirty two-seaters were ordered with deliveries commencing in late 1969 to 313 Squadron at Twenthe. This squadron became the conversion unit and trained pilots to equip the following squadrons: 314 at

Below: A two-seater NF-5B of the training unit 313 Squadron landing at Bruggen. This aircraft has since been sold to Turkey.

Eindhoven, 315 at Twenthe and 316 at Gilze-Rijen. The NF-5 fleet is gradually being replaced by the F-16, with 313 and 315 having converted so far. The remaining squadrons, 314 and 316 have also recently swapped bases, with 316 now in residence at Eindhoven. Next to convert will be 314, who should have started as these words are written. These units should have converted to the F-16 by 1992, and disposal of the NF-5 fleet has already begun to Turkey and Venezuela.

Opposite: This 314 Squadron NF-5A was photographed whilst taking part in the 1988 NATO Tactical Air Meet at Sollingen.

Below: A 314 Squadron NF-5A in an attractive blue camouflage scheme.

Opposite: Loaded down with three long range fuel tanks, this 313 Squadron NF-5A lands at Waddington where it was deployed for a NATO exercise. In the past few years some of the Dutch NF-5 fleet have received a low visibility grey paint scheme.

Below: The golden centaur of 314 Squadron stands out well on the old camouflage scheme of this NF-5A on the runway at Bruggen.

Opposite: In pristine condition and minus unit markings, this aircraft, K-3001, was the first Dutch NF-5A. It spent most of its life with the Test Group at Twenthe, but is currently on the strength of 314 Squadron.

Below: An NF-5B of 314 Squadron about to touch down at Fairford.

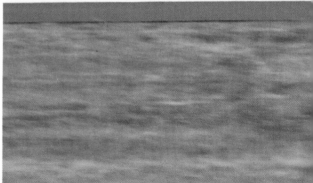

Opposite: This 315 Squadron NF-5A wears patriotic red/white/blue markings for the 1980 display season.

Below: A regular attraction during the airshow season is the Dutch solo NF-5 display. The aircraft selected is usually painted like this 314 Squadron machine, specially for the season.

Opposite: A pair of grey painted 316 Squadron aircraft rotate from the Sollingen runway. Note the aircraft nearest the camera is devoid of unit markings.

Below: K-3017, a 316 Squadron NF-5A departs Abingdon carrying a baggage pod on the centreline pylon.

Overleaf: Snapped as the tyres are about to make contact with the Bruggen runway, K-3025 is an NF-5A of 315 Squadron from Twenthe.

Opposite: Photographed on the runway at Greenham Common is 315 Squadron NF-5A K-3019. The aircraft was participating in the 1981 International Air Tattoo, hence the attractive, specially applied paint scheme.

Below: Decelerating with the aid of a brake parachute is an NF-5A of 316 Squadron in an all over grey scheme.

NORWAY

An early customer for the F-5 Freedom Fighter was the Royal Norwegian Air Force (RNoAF), who received their first aircraft in 1966. A total of 108 aircraft were delivered to equip six squadrons, most of whom were previously flying the F-86 Sabre. First recipient was 336 Skvadron at Rygge, followed by No. 332 at the same base, and eventually 334 (Bodo), 338 (Oerland), 717 (Rygge) and 718 (Sola) followed. Of these, 717 flew the RF-5A, whilst 718, being the training unit, received the bulk of the two seater F-5Bs. Due to a higher than average loss rate and the introduction of the F-16, the F-5 fleet has been run down considerably, with 336 Skvadron the only remaining unit. A number of aircraft have also been disposed of to Greece and Turkey.

Below: All the Norwegian F-5Bs have been through an update programme to extend their lives, and this is perhaps the reason that this aircraft of 336 Skvadron looks so immaculate. Only one of the fourteen F-5Bs delivered has been lost, and all the survivors serve with 336. Very few of the unit's aircraft carry unit markings these days.

Opposite: Sixteen RF-5A reconnaissance variants were delivered to 717 Skvadron at Rygge; the sole operator until its disbandment in 1980. Thereafter the recce birds were flown by 336 Skvadron, who operated a large fleet of all three models received by the RNoAF. Norway has now retired all its RF-5As, and six have been transferred to the Turkish Air Force. Illustrated is an RF-5A in 336 Skvadron markings.

Below: Norwegian F-5s carry only the last three digits of their USAF serial numbers, as seen on this 336 Skvadron F-5B at Bruggen.

Opposite: Oerland Air Base near Trondheim is home to 338 Skvadron, which was the last Norwegian unit to convert to the F-16. As an F-5 unit 338 Skvadron aircraft were rare visitors to Britsh airfields, though F-5A '224' was photographed during a visit to Wyton.

Below: With the camouflaged hangar and snow on the ground this photograph could only have been taken in Norway. Despite the absence of unit markings this F-5A belongs to 338 Skvadron at Oerland where the shot was taken. One or two Norwegian F-5s were applied with a green camouflage scheme as an experiment — which was never taken up, hence the colour of the drop tanks.

Below: When the RF-5As were on the strength of 717 Skvadron they always seemed to be devoid of unit markings, as was the case when this aircraft was photographed landing at Bruggen. This aircraft has since been transferred to the Turkish Air Force.

SPAIN

The Spanish Air Force received seventy F-5s license built by CASA. These were split as follows: thirty-four two seat SF-5Bs and eighteen each of the SF-5A and SRF-5A variants, contrary to many sources which wrongly quote nineteen and seventeen respectively. The bulk of the two seater variant went to 202 and 204 Escuadrones which formed the training wing; Escuela de Reactores at Talavera la Real. These later became 731 and 732

Escuadrones of Ala 73, and more recently changed again to 231 and 232 Escuadrones of Ala 23. At Moron 211 and 212 Escuadrones were equipped with all three variants in the ground attack role. Before long, however, 212 Escuadron disbanded, and its aircraft were sent to Gando in the Canary Islands where it reformed as 464 Escuadron. Eventually these events were reversed, and on disbandment of 464, 212 was again reformed alongside 211 Escuadron in Ala 21, and both units remain current at Moron.

Below: SF-5B from 732 Escuadron in the clear blue skies over Western Spain.

Overleaf: An Escuela de Reactores F-5B displays its upper surfaces to the camera.

Opposite: An SF-5B of the Escuela de Reactores 732 Escuadron in a climbing turn whilst on a training flight from Talavera. The 'cotton wool' underneath is not clouds — but fog, a far from common event in Spain.

Below: This Ala 21 SF-5B looks immaculate, having just come out of the paint shop at Moron.

Opposite: A 732 Escuadron SF-5B breaking away from the lead aircraft over a Spanish countryside shrouded in fog.

Below: The unit badge of 211 Escuadron. Sister unit, 212 Escuadron, has the same badge but with a green background.

Opposite: An SF-5B diving earthwards at a great rate of knots. Northrop's nimble lightweight is a delight to fly in.

Below: Rather weather beaten and badly in need of a coat of paint, this 212 Escuadron SF-5A was photographed at Zaragoza where it was deployed to use the nearby weapons ranges.

Overleaf: The SRF-5As of Ala 21 complement the RF-4C Phantoms of Ala 12 in providing a reconnaissance capability to the Mando de la Aviacion Tactica (Tactical Air Command). This aircraft of 212 Escuadron was photographed on take-off from its base at Moron. Note the reduced size of the national insignia on the rudder compared to the Talavera based non-camouflaged aircraft.

Opposite: An SF-5A of Ala 21 taxies clear of its parking slot on the Moron flightline.

Below: The author airborne in a Spanish SF-5B.

Below: With undercarriage retracting, this 212 Escuadron SF-5B climbs
out of Moron Air Base.

SWITZERLAND

The Swiss Flugwaffe selected the F-5E as a replacement for the veteran de Havilland Venoms in the ground attack role. The programme was given the U.S. code name 'Peace Alps', and the first aircraft were delivered to Emmen by C-5 Galaxy. The order comprised sixty-six F-5E and six F-5F models, with a repeat order accounting for a further thirty-two Es and six Fs. The Swiss Tiger IIs are equipped with AIM-9 Sidewinders for their secondary role of air defence, complementing the Mirage III fleet. The Swiss are rather reticent at disclosing details of their order of battle. However the following Fliegerstaffeln (Squadrons) operate the F-5; 1, 6, 8, 11, 13, 18 and 19. Of these, numbers 6, 8, 13 and 19 are militia units flown by reservists. In peacetime Tigers operate from the main bases at Dubendorf and Payerne, but are frequently seen operating from other locations, such as Alpnach, Interlaken, Meiringen and Sion, and can operate from other wartime bases, as well as the autobahns.

Below: Aircraft from the second batch built featured a new flattened, more streamlined nosecone, as seen on this aircraft of Fliegerstaffel 1. The remainder of the fleet is also being fitted with the new nose.

Overleaf: A pair of Flugwaffe F-5Es on approach to Dubendorf Air Base on the outskirts of Zurich. The lead aircraft carries the marking of Fliegerstaffel 13.

Opposite: An F-5E wearing the Tiger insignia of Fliegerstaffel 11 taxies clear of the runway at Dubendorf.

Below: All Swiss Tigers are in the two tone air superiority grey colour scheme as seen on this Fliegerstaffel 11 F-5E on final approach to Dubendorf.

Opposite: As aircraft are frequently rotated between bases many Swiss F-5s do not carry unit markings, unlike this machine of Fliegerstaffel 19, which is believed to operate from Alpnach in time of war.

Below: this F-5E of Fliegerstaffel 13 still has the 'old' nosecone. This unit is comprised of reservists, many of whom are Swissair pilots.

Opposite: This F-5E, J-3014, was the first one to be assembled by the Federal Aircraft Factory at Emmen, and has since been fitted with the new nosecone. With Fliegerstaffel 18 insignia on the nose it was photographed at its Dubendorf base.

Below: The unit insignia on the nose of this F-5E identifies it as belonging to Fliegerstaffel 18.

Below: An F-5F devoid of unit marks at Payerne.

TURKEY

An early customer for the F-5 Freedom Fighter, Turkey began to receive aircraft at the same time as its NATO ally Greece. The Turk Hava Kuvvetleri (Turkish Air Force) received a total of 110 aircraft, comprising seventy-seven F-5A, twenty RF-5A and thirteen F-5Bs. These were delivered to 161 and 163 Filo (Squadron) at Bandirma, 142

Overleaf: This camouflage scheme is definitely not standard Turkish Air Force pattern. This F-5B is a recent acquisition from the USAF. *(Aad Wever)*

Below: Early build F-5A from 5 Jet Base at Merzifon.

and 143 Filo at Merzifon and 192 Filo at Balikesir. A reorganisation of the Air Force in 1971, however, meant a number of units being renumbered. At Bandirma 163 Filo became 162, whilst at Merzifon 142 and 143 became 151 and 152. More recently the THK has received a glut of F-5s, including a few ex-USAF F-5Bs, and over thirty F-5A and RF-5As from Norway, whilst the first of sixty Dutch machines have been delivered. Units currently operating the type are: 133 Filo at No. 3 Jet Base, Konya; 151, 152 and 153 Filo at No. 5 Jet Base, Merzifon; and 183 Filo at No. 8 Jet Base, Diyarbakir, the latter being equipped with the RF-5A.

Below: With cockpit transparencies covered by brown paper, this F-5A is towed to the spray shop at the overhaul facility at Eskisehir. The aircraft belongs to 5 Jet Base at Merzifon.

AFRICA

The Kenya Air Force ordered ten F-5E and two F-5Fs in 1976, the only other jet ever to be operated by this air arm

Below: A Kenya Air Force F-5E photographed on a test flight prior to delivery. *(Northrop)*

being the BAC167 Strikemaster. Following an attempted coup in 1982, the Air Force now comes under Army control, and is known as the '82 Air Force. The F-5s operate from the main base at Laikipia formerly known as Nanyuki.

Overleaf: The Sudan Air Force took delivery of two F-5Fs in 1982, with ten F-5Es following two years later. The two seaters were photographed on delivery through Prestwick. *(Pete Smith)*

Opposite: The first F-5F for the Kenya AF on its delivery flight through Prestwick *(Pete Smith)*

Below: Morocco operated both the F-5A and B models from its base at Kenitra, and these were supplemented by a small number of ex-Iranian machines including two RF-5A reconnaissance variants. Some of these remain operational, and the F-5 fleet has been expanded by the delivery of sixteen E and four F models in 1981. These have seen action against Polisario guerrillas. Recently, a small number of ex-Alconbury based USAF F-5Es have been delivered. Illustrated is an F-5E in desert camouflage. *(GB Aircraft Slides)*

The Tunisian Air Force ordered F-5s in 1982, and soon afterwards took delivery of eight E and four F models. These have since been supplemented by seven ex-USAF F-5Es from Alconbury.

Below: Tunisian F-5E in an attractive camouflage scheme on delivery through Alconbury.

ASIA

The largest operator of the F-5 today is Taiwan's Republic of China Air Force (ROCAF). It has received in excess of 400 aircraft, including over 300 Tiger IIs license built by AIDC. During the conflict in Vietnam forty-eight F-5As were lent to the SVNAF, and some of the survivors were returned at the end of the war. Known F-5E/F units are: 1 TFW at Tainan, 2 TFW at Hsin Chu, 5 CW at Taoyuan and the 455 TFW at Chiayi. Other F-5 bases are Ching Chuan Kang, Hualien and Taitung, the latter believed to be home to the remaining F-5A/B variants.

Below: Sixty-six two seater F-5Fs were license built by AIDC. This one was photographed at a defence exhibition at Taipei/Sungshan airport.

The task of air defence of Indonesian territory is under-taken by one unit of Tiger IIs, this being 14 Skwadron, 300 Wing of the Tentara Nasional Indonesia — Angkatan Udara (TNI-AU). This translates to Indonesian Air Force, and the unit which comprises eight E and four F models is located at Iswahyudi AFB, Madiun, which is on the large island of Java.

Opposite: One of 14 Skwadron's colourful F-5Es photographed at Jakarta/Kemayoran airport.

Below: Markings of 300 Wing TNI-AU on an F-5E.

Above: Unit insignia of 14 Skwadron TNI-AU.

The Republic of Korea Air Force (ROKAF) still operates a large fleet of the Northrop fighter and, apart from the RF-5E which it never received, all variants are still in its inventory. Modest numbers of the A and B models operate alongside 149 E and fifty F variants, some of which were license built. The country is absolutely paranoid about security, and photography is prohibited at Seoul's international airport, and at one of the main tourist attractions, the revolving restaurant on top of the Seoul tower in the middle of the city, similar to the CN Tower in Toronto. For this reason details of ROKAF units are unreliable, but they are believed to be as follows: at Kwangju the 1 TFW comprises 115, 122 and 123 TFS, Suwon has the 10 TFW with the 102, and 105 TFS, plus one other unit, whilst the squadron resident at Kunsan is believed to be the 111 TFS.

Opposite: A number of ROKAF F-5Es have recently adopted an all over grey scheme as seen on this aircraft landing at Osan. The unit insignia underneath the cockpit is believed to be that of the 111 TFS at Kunsan.

Above: Northrop built ROKAF F-5E in USAF Vietnam-type tactical camouflage scheme. *(Northrop)*

The Tentara Udara Diraja Malaysia (TUDM), which translates to Royal Malaysian Air Force, uses the F-5E in the air defence role from the former Australian base at Butterworth. These are operated by Nos. 11 and 12 Squadrons. The TUDM initially received two F-5Bs, but these have since been sold to Thailand, and eventually a total of seventeen E, four F and two RF-5Es were delivered.

Opposite: An 11 Squadron F-5E at Butterworth. *(David Oliver)*

Above: Malaysia was the first customer for the RF-5E Tigereye with an order for two, the second of which is illustrated prior to delivery.
(GB Aircraft Slides)

An early customer for the F-5A was the Philippines Air Force which received nineteen A and three B Models to equip the 6 TFS of the 5 FW at Basa. The first aircraft arrived in 1965 to replace F-86 Sabres in the air defence role. They were later supplemented by F-8H Crusaders, which have since been retired, leaving the F-5s as the sole jet fighter in the Phil.AF. inventory. Attrition has been heavy, and only eight A and two B models remain at the time of writing. It is likely however that the USAF F-5Es of the 26 AS will be handed over to the Phil.AF. now that they have been replaced by the F-16.

Opposite: The Cobra insignia of the 6 TFS Phil.AF.

Opposite: The Blue Diamonds aerobatic team used the F-86 until replaced by the F-5A. The team gave its last performance with the F-5 in the mid 1980s, hence the shabby paintwork on this aircraft.

Below: one of the two remaining F-5Bs of the Phil. AF.

Above: In 1987 the Phil.AF. started to give its F-5 fleet a badly needed overhaul and coat of paint, as seen on these 6 TFS aircraft on the Basa flightline.

One of the most modern and well equipped air arms in South East Asia is that of Singapore. With the possible exception of Vietnam, this tiny state is surrounded by friendly countries, yet has a large fleet of well over one hundred A-4, F-5, F-16 and Hunter combat aircraft, and E-2 Hawkeye surveillance aircraft. This inventory of primarily offensive aircraft, added to its absolute paranoia about security, must be making some of its neighbours extremely anxious. The Republic of Singapore Air Force is believed to have received thirty-six F-5Es — including the last batch built, and ten F-5Fs. These are operated by 144 'Lynx' Squadron at Paya Lebar and 149 'Shirkra' Squadron at Tengah, and if rumours are to be believed, underground hangars have been built at the latter.

Opposite: This 144 Squadron F-5E was photographed on a rare visit to the Malaysian base at Butterworth where it was participating in an exercise. (David Oliver)

Opposite: Singapore F-5s can be seen in this 'jungle' type camouflage or an overall grey scheme. This aircraft of 149 Squadron was photographed at Butterworth in Malaysia. *(David Oliver)*

Below: An F-5F of 149 Squadron landing at Clark AB.

Above: The last three F-5Es built by Northrop seen on delivery through Prestwick en-route to the Singapore Air Force. *(Pete Smith)*

Deliveries of F-5A/B models to the Royal Thai Air Force initially went to 13 Squadron at Don Muang, which later relocated to Nakhom Ratchasima (formerly known as Korat) and became 103 Squadron. The unit flies the survivors of twenty-four A, four RF-5A and two F-5Bs supplied under MAP, and two B models acquired from Malaysia. Later deliveries comprised thirty-two new E and six F models from the Northrop production line, and a further ten ex-USAF F-5Es. Nakhom Ratchasima is home to the 1st Fighter Wing, comprising 102 and 103 Squadrons, the former operating the newer F-5E. The remaining squadron, which also operates the E model, is 403 Squadron of 4 Fighter Wing at Ta Khli.

Opposite: Wearing colourful aggressor type markings this F-5E belongs to 102 'Cobra' Squadron, and was photographed at a display at Don Muang. *(Chris Pocock)*

Below: An F-5A of 103 'Tiger' Squadron Royal Thai Air Force.
(Chris Pocock)

LATIN AMERICA

The largest air arm in South America, the Forca Aerea Brasileira (FAB) uses the Tiger II to supplement its Mirage III force in the air defence role. Thirty-six F-5Es were delivered to equip 1 and 2 Esquadrao of the 1st Fighter Group at Santa Cruz. Rather strangely, the four two-seaters bought were B rather than F models. The FAB Tiger IIs have refuelling probes fitted to enable them to be in-flight refuelled by Boeing KC-137 and Lockheed KC-130 tankers. Acceptance of ex-USAF aircraft has just been completed, comprising twenty-four E and four F variants.

Overleaf: Equipped with AIM-9 Sidewinder missiles, the first FAB F-5E is illustrated on a test flight. *(Northrop)*

Below: A USAF F-5F destined for Brazil with dual markings on the fin. *(Maurice Bertrand)*

Opposite: In 1981 the Fuerza Aerea Mexicana (FAM) ordered ten F-5Es and two Fs to equip 401 Escuadron at Santa Lucia for air defence duties. The only other jet combat aircraft in the FAM inventory were ageing AT-33 armed trainers. Illustrated is an FAM F-5F. *(Northrop)*

Below: The Fuerza Aerea de Chile (FAC) accepted its first F-5E in 1976, eventually receiving fifteen E and three F models to equip 7 Grupo at Antofagasta. These aircraft, like many export Tiger IIs had a dorsal fin fillet for improved manoeuvrability and a VHF blade aerial on the spine, as seen in this view of a 7 Grupo F-5E. *(Northrop)*

Below: The bulk of ex-USAF aircraft delivered have come from the 425 TFTS at Williams AFB. One of the aircraft destined for the FAB was photographed on the Williams ramp prior to delivery to Brazil, wearing both FAB and USAF markings. *(Maurice Bertrand)*

MIDDLE EAST

The Royal Jordanian Air Force (RJAF) has been a member of the F-5 club for many years, initially receiving thirty A and six B models from the IIAF. Fifteen of these have since

Overleaf: A desert camouflaged F-5E of 9 Squadron RJAF.

Below: A pair of RJAF F-5Es which participated in the 1981 International Air Tattoo at Greenham Common.

been handed on to the Greek Air Force, the remainder serving with 6 Squadron at Mafraq. Numbers 1, 2 and 5 Squadrons also at some stage operated the F-5A. A sizeable force of Tiger IIs have been delivered, and equip 9 and 17 Squadrons at Prince Hassan Air Base, formerly known as H5. Another F-5E unit, No. 11 Squadron at Azraq, is believed to have converted to the Mirage F1.

Above: Heavily loaded with three long range fuel tanks, this F-5E of 9 Squadron RJAF has the nose leg extended by three degrees to decrease the take-off run.

Well over one hundred Tiger IIs equip the Royal Saudi Air Force (RSAF) whilst most of the twenty F-5Bs delivered in 1973 remain on the inventory. Tiger IIs currently serve with 3 and 10 Squadrons at Taif, 15 at Khamis Mushayt and 17 at Tabuk. A previous operator, 7 Squadron at Dhahran, has re-equipped with the Tornado. The RSAF was the second and final customer for the RF-5E Tigereye with an order for ten aircraft for 17 Squadron.

Opposite: An RF-5E Tigereye in Saudi desert camouflage scheme.
(Pete Smith)

Overleaf: The last new customer for Northrop's lightweight fighter was the Bahrain Amiri Air Force who took delivery in 1988 of eight E and four F models. This was the first fixed wing aircraft for the air arm of this Persian Gulf island. These four aircraft were photographed staging through Prestwick en-route to Bahrain's International airport at Muharraq.
(Pete Smith)

Below: At least one RF-5E has been painted in an all-black scheme, and was photographed staging through Prestwick on delivery. Note that this aircraft has a refuelling probe to enable it to refuel from RSAF C-130 and KE-3 tanker aircraft. *(Pete Smith)*